SPECIAL THANKS

Special thanks to my wife
for giving me the inspiration and support to follow my dreams

Special thanks to my daughter
for making me a father

Special thanks to my parents
for instilling in me the collaborative role that family and education
has in the development of bright young minds

Special thanks to you for buying my book and promoting positivity to
our young girls of color.

TO:

FROM:

The inspiration for this project came directly from the birth of Briar Lawrence's daughter Nile. He knew he would read to his daughter, and wanted the first words he read to her to set the pace for the lifelong bond he would share with her. This project is a celebration of the father and daughter relationship, as well as a children's book. *Little Brown Girl* is written intentionally to be read by a father figure to a daughter to facilitate a bond based on literacy, spirituality, cultural awareness and active engagement.

LITTLE BROWN GIRL

By Brian Lawrence
For Nile Elizabeth Brown-Lawrence

♥

Illustrations by Precious Beast

Little Brown Girl, you were not even born before you started changing my world. When I learned of your arrival I felt a level of love, responsibility, and happiness that I would not trade for any amount of riches or gold.

Little Brown Girl, I'm your father and you have given me a very special job to do.
As one of your parents, I'm here to help you understand God's plan and make sure you see it through.

Little Brown Girl, we will pray every day and live out God's commandments right because there may be times when only prayer and God's word will guide you out of darkness to the light.

Nile

Little Brown Girl, I'm here to tell you that your Brown represents beauty that flows from your head to the floor, but you must understand your brand of Brown represents so much more.

Little Brown Girl, do not feel slighted when I focus my praise on your intellect, character, and spirit. " You are more than beautiful " will leave my lips any time you need to hear it.

Little Brown Girl, I will teach you to live in your skin with dignity, honor, and pride.

I promise that even when you misbehave I will instill discipline without putting a hand to your behind.

Nile

Little Brown Girl, I promise to spend time with you and be active in anything you want to do or play, so as long as you at least try basketball, because I have to teach you my crossover and how to shoot the jay

Little Brown Girl, one day you will leave our house and take yourself to school and I want you to understand it's more important to surround yourself with those who are creative and scholarly rather than those more concerned with popularity and being cool.

Little Brown Girl, your education and leadership will work together to form a skeleton key - use it to open all doors of understanding; who you are, where you are going, and what your impact on the world will be.

Little Brown Girl, there have been Brown Women who broke down barriers so you can be a torch carrier.

Brown Women that didn't accept no, in order to change your status quo, and those who uprooted social weeds to meet your social needs.

Little Brown Girl...

Just like Harriet Tubman, Phillis Wheatley, and Madame C.J. Walker, you must strive to be a difference maker every single day.

Like Josephine Baker, Shirley Chisholm, and Maya Angelou, you must have an unwavering belief in your goals and dreams even when no one else around believes in them but you.

Like Mary McCloud Bethune, Mae Jemison, and Condoleezza Rice, develop your mind into your most valuable commodity and know its worth can't be measured by price

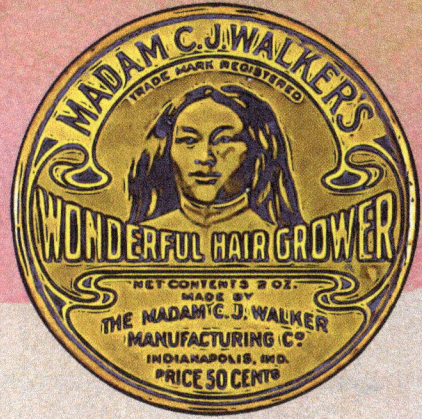

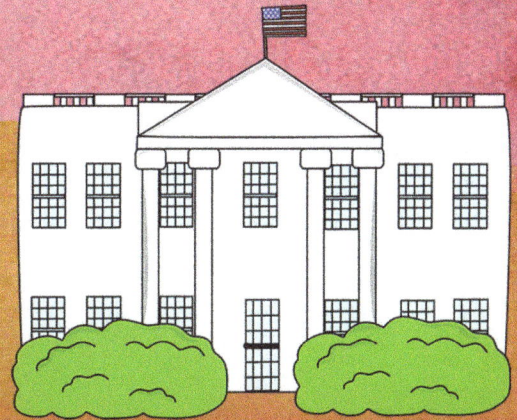

Little Brown Girl, just like every on
of those great women who fought
the good fight and whose blood
flowed red starting life as Little
Brown Girls will always be you and
their common thread.

Brian Lawrence is a father, educator and author. He began his writing career three years ago as a content contributor for *goodgirlradio.com* and the *gentlemenhood.com* with one goal in mind celebrating women and children of color. Brian's creativity is largely informed by the responsibility he feels to make content that promotes literacy, helps build self-esteem and encourages cultural awareness. Any project that has his name on it will inspire people of color and help them embrace their individuality, strengthen their talents and stimulate cultural pride.